Trotting With
The Fox

Trotting With The Fox

Poems

Dick Heaberlin

Orange House Books
San Marcos, Texas

For additional information visit the author's website at DickHeaberlinWrites.com.

Copyright 2009 by Dick Heaberlin

ISBN 978-0-9794964-6-2

For Andrea

Contents

Material Matters	9
Conjunction	10
Autumn's Touch	11
Against the Gray	12
Her Autumn	13
Housewarming	14
Green Valentine	15
Mum	16
Transcendent	17
Definition	18
En un tiempo de la llaneza	19
Orange, Texas 1943	20
Infant's Night	21
Fireflies	22
Out Back Back Then	23
Christmas 1978	24
The Staples Store	25
Las Cruces, 1964	26
Rooted	28
Leftovers	29
Roosting	30
Cowman	31
Caution	32
Again	33

Elisa	34
Grooming	35
Sheen	36
Prana	37
Across Dawn's Edge	38
Refuge	39
Invitation to Dance	40
Disjunction	42
Just Judy	43
A Man of Style	44
Flash of Summer	45
In the Shade	46
Life List #404	48
Poet	49
Oliver and the Rock	50
For Sure	51
More, More	52
Stuff	53
Midwinter Lambing	54
Among Sheep	55
In a Grey Suit	56
Puffery	57

Material Matters

That

blend of cotton

and silk

in torch tones

changing toward sky

moving against moves

with them

soft dance

of rays syncopated

onto night

squirming light

pinkly

orange toward pleasure

intricate weave

tenderly worked.

Conjunction

Beneath the gray stone

wall of the nunnery

we stood

and said

we'd do.

Autumn's Touch

In the early evenings

of October,

the sun knocks at our door.

Andrea is here.

She invites it in,

and it spreads out

across the floor,

long and invading and slow,

bronzing things.

Against the Gray

I've not seen a red fox

warm in this gray stone arroyo

not seen it trot

through Spanish oak leaves.

But I've seen her here,

with me,

lighted,

flaming bronze

against the gray of rocks

and green of cedar.

Her Autumn

It's October and November again
Andrea's best time,
cooling some, at last,
and time for the fall shows —
Antiques at Comfort, Castroville, Round Top —
not needing to buy
but seeing, feeling, even fondling
some warm old pine bench,
her hand moving softly across its age,
it from a Kentucky school, well-worn
by mountain children.
I think of Jesse Stuart and Greenup County.

And time for the other fall show
all those burning Autumn colors —
zinnias in yellow, orange, bronze
and mums, too
and crepe myrtle leaves,
turning — some becoming yellow
others coral, almost red.

Her best time, for she is lit by and lights them
and my time, too,
to shine gold in her Autumn glow.

Housewarming

I like the way
the nice small
steady fire
keeps burning
in our hearth.

Green Valentine

With the rain
funny how instantly
it's so much greener,
the moss on the long leaning wedding oak
coming brightly erect,
emeralds for Andrea.

Mum

We make no mistake,
watch a flower,
ours.
It's bronze
and gold
and rolls
in the light.
Yes, we shall watch,
smile
kiss cheeks lightly
hold the green stem.

Transcendent

I like the way

you spread

the sky

around me.

Definition

Out here in the rock and oak
we have more moon.
Its light sits on the trees
coaxing,

"Break from cover."

We
will go
bare
into the meadow
to be silvered.

En un tiempo de la llaneza

Esta nochebuena
cualquiera flor
vemos
nos gusta
aqui en San Miguel.
Cualquiera cosa
hacemos
nos gusta
aqui en San Miguel.
Todos nos gusta
mientras que vivimos
bajo del sol
mientras que vivimos
unidos,
Andrea y yo,
aqui en San Miguel.

Orange, Texas 1943

The dog

sank its growl

into my day.

I dropped my syrup

can of crawdads,

the butter,

salt,

matches,

everything.

The crawdads crawled off

like slow sun rays.

The dog held me

with stiff circles,

bristles,

left me soft shook,

an old shoe.

Infant's Night

Almost diaphanous

pink fingers

tiny tendrils

reach for light

weaving

seeking meticulously

caring

soft pads

would draw chaos

mouthward.

Fireflies

(Orange, Texas; 1950)

Last place
of fire flight
spot in black
there,
not there,
spirit of spark—
held shortly
in me
to blend
with new flash—
be swallowed
in it.
Who and what
was what? Now?
Sandra,
Betty Sue?

Out Back Back Then

The bearded man with delving eyes had cast
his stare across my path, had strewn black cats
about, had sent me spinning back somewhere
to grab her gingham apron starchly there.

And too his dog, huge Chow it was, so black
with purple tongue and devil grin, sat back
and watched from picket pen me play so near;
through the tiny slot I knew it knew my fear.

And I still see his alligator gar,
Oh, yes, so stinky dead, those teeth,
and snout, and eyes with perpetual stare,
rotting in his yard, a smell beneath
his willow tree; and whirl I'd go and seek
to find her touch, for me, small and meek.

Christmas 1978

Oh, Joan, freshly combed

cleaned and garbed in green

so newly grown to mirrors

combs and colognes.

Oh, Joan, suddenly thirteen

with soft voice and skin

newly noticing boys

though still quick with tears.

The Staples Store

Staples had a store.
Thin
silver-haired men
sat
slowly
slicing
slivers
of life
from gnarled sticks.

Las Cruces, 1964

In a sandyard in a desert

Aunt Sally Dunaway,

eighty-nine,

whose calloused hands

firm back

force the earth tight

about juniper post—

a bob of printed bonnet,

post to post,

so slow—

lift, drop, pat, pack

under fine sky

swirling sun.

Perhaps her mind

covered her with pine,

sweetgum,

sent her away

to time of

chop,

pick,

red-iron soil

to Rusk, Gladewater, Nacogdoches,

to damp hot morning

cotton shirtwaist

grimed flesh,

soft,

sun hurting,

to buttermilk, blackeyes, corn bread.

First and last light

a small force in the cotton field,

tinier now,

bent.

Yet the posts,

packed tight,

rise straight,

in the desert.

Rooted

Beans curling in the stingy heat,
drying quietly, ground cracked,
sun coming down,
nobody here but me,
rocking quietly
with my good sweet tea,
that doily getting yellow,
and that hen that won't stay home,
just like Ella, all them kids,
where'd I put the pictures,
hot, whew,
sweat, and rocking, and tea
and beans curling in the stingy heat.

Leftovers

In Shiloh

some yellow doilies

cracking acquer.

Flowered wall paper

peeling,

mildewed.

On the table

cold biscuits.

gravy.

A rocker s squeak.

squeak.

squeak.

Ella watching

for specks —

dust

in sunrays.

Roosting

The two from Michigan move,

old heads white as Winter ptarmigans,

along the resaca

on the asphalt circle

the waddle of old fat pooch before,

move stiffly, softly, quietly

to Chacalaca noise

exploding —

a cacophony in the half light.

And closeby a man

newly baptized

rises from the Rio Grande.

The Airstreams reflect

rich purples, pinks, oranges

flamboyant as Tropical Kingbirds,

Altamira Orioles.

A green jay squawks.

Then the warm dark.

Cowman

A dust crusted

old one

though gaunt

from long going

still ajingle.

Caution

Blind man on a horse,
stirring up clouds
old man of circles
choking on dust
spurring.
Old man on a horse
going round
blindly proud
watch the sword.

Again

Magical words slip in
come gliding—
comfort, pallet, quilt—

soft sleepy words
to bed down on
come grating—
iron bedstead, pail, bob wire,
staples, nails, skillet—

words abrasive
as Winter bedsteads

memory words
to draw me home

magic carpet words
to make what was before
again.

Elisa

Flowers have a way,

those insistent

powerful flowers

brash

confident

flashing bright

to lure the beaks

and tongues of green

and black-chinned birds,

seeking the intruders

vitally.

Grooming

I spend my days
looking at my trees—
mentally
climbing them
taking off a twig or limb
here and there.
Sometimes
I actually trim them.
They will stand
as still as a poodle
being prepared
for the show ring
while I scratch their stomach,
tickle their ear,
talk to 'em,
say, "Good tree."

Sheen

I breathed
on a bronze thing
saw my breath there
light
palpable.

With a soft green cotton cloth
I glossed
essentially.

Prana

Though near dark early

he sees the wind

there

in the grass

and would breathe it home —

would draw it by the trees

and the trees are fuzzy

with leaves

squeezing squirming curling out

would coax it by these breathing trees

into a simple room.

Across Dawn's Edge

We try to talk about
how across the edge of dawn
we see and hear
the wind and light and form of things.
We try to
but come out empty-mouthed
tongue-snubbed
while seeing the metamorphic light
bring,
in a blink,
new forms, new things newly lit
newly colored —
a green,
glowing
with violet and gold —
try and fail to find words
and settle for,
with a smile,
the shapes and sounds
we have,
settle for this bird,
beating —
from the juniper grove,
suddenly,
bursting.

Refuge

In blue June, things
are thickest.
There's rain.
Live Oaks are full
above heavy shadows.
Some think the ground
lacy
in the deep places.
There's marsh too
with soft
tight dark
closed away
from quick
light,
bald cypress and moss
a place
for the
small scared
the warblers
for subtle
flickerings
of gray
in the blue
and music
fired from
cover.

Invitation to Dance

In warm Maine, 1890.
Hanga-like, Hiroshigian dancing figures of the night.
No moon, but its silver
flashing
on purple blue,
its silver
dancing
across dancing waters.
  Come out tonight.

America's Homer
his dancing mind
its dancing hands
artist's moving weapons against movement
hands which dare dance

watched from a point
to
fix
fast
the moment beach it land it,
bring it to shore
for the watchers
to view consume

hold nature the dancers
for
their consideration..

Won't you come out tonight
  come out tonight
to dance, to watch,
to watch the dancers, the watchers.

The dancing figures
hands upraised, outflung, interlaced
lighted by lantern.

Those watchers he watched
purple appreciater critics
silhouetted against silver
spinning always like the fog light.
It,
fixed in one red moment
pointed human light come ashore
from distant island.
  Come out tonight.

Disjunction

Michael,
Michael,
you, who were so here—
so suddenly gone,
we stay—
puzzled
passionate in our loss,
less
since denied you.

Just Judy

She was fine,
she said,
fine,
cancered and fine.
Praying.

Judy was just fine.
Paralyzed and praying and fine.
Strange to us, fine?
She said no pain, no fear, no worry.
Fine, just fine.

A Man of Style

Because he was he,
Ralph,
gentle, patient,
attentive,
knowledgeable
and because
he
folded
and unfolded
his words
neatly, tellingly
we believed
and were glad we did.

Flash of Summer

To startle sunrays,
jar them off their way,
force them
to rebound,
there is a russet elk
on a hill shining,
green and red stripes
of a trout,
a hawk up high,
rain on pines,
a prismic dew on raspberries
— something to shatter light
    drop it

    like broken bulbs
        on an oak floor
aspen leaves shaking
rays around,
sending them swirling,
a flurry of
hot Summer snowflakes.

In the Shade

Green and cool are His plants—

fir, black gum, pine,

redwood, wisteria vine.

West of San Rafael, coastal

redwoods let little slits

of sun slip through, minute

bits within a canopy of shade.

Jonah loved God's gourd.

Along Cow bayou near the Sabine

beneath Cypress trees, and amidst

the grotesque knees, steaming light

slides across black swamp water.

Beneath long leaf and loblolly pine,

boy scouts sing

"Green grow the rushes, ho."

Jonah wanted shade.

And East of Alamogordo

high in the Sacramentos

Douglas fir and blue spruce

coolly cover the rocky soil

allowing occasional rays

to dart through.

I, like Jonah, want shade,

want protection, need a Deity

to intercede, to come between

nature and me, to darken the

Sun, its radiance, its heat,

its naked burning purity,

to reflect its heat from me.

Life List #404

Bob O'Connor said Scott got a condor,
saw it soar, really,
first it was along the horizon's fringe,
then its pace was curbed, slow, slower,
till it fluffed down onto a leather-seated Mercedes.
He said it was midday, in the desert,
and there was gold on gold on gold
—sun splinters.

Then Bob said Scott went to Texas to get an Ivory-billed woodpecker or a golden-cheeked warbler, maybe number 405.

Bob thinks Scott's an odd miser.

Poet

He's the clown

who throws flowers,

goes around

on his word

pedaling crazed,

paint on his face,

double smile.

Oliver and the Rock

I see in the space
where the rock was

the rock

still there
still feel me moving it
feel it moving
feel me feeling

then

and now

see and feel that

just by seeing the space
where the rock was
and isn't.

For Sure

To know for sure,
I'd like that, to see
what's straight
to select the proper cue,
   proper shot,
to know what's what.

Yeah, a lot of us
would like that,
to know what to plant,
Big Boys or Spring Giant,
know what nematodes know,
the best? What'll burn,
what'll bloom?
What is good,
What to use,
   to know of cause, and means,
   and who.
Why did Faustus choose Helen, not Isolde,
or, or. . . a million other whos?

What to cut away, what to take in?
Oh, for sure!

More, More

I want a lot,

a red, blue and green

and one of those pink ones,

please dig in deep, and orange too.

I want a lot.

Oh, please!

Stuff

The intricate web
binding stuff
to the consequential
is tissue thin
easy to rip
when need or wish
steps bigfootedly in.
Stuff falls out,
lies neglected
like a tow sack of meowling kittens
along a country road.
But stuff lovers notice
though slow to come
when they come
they come rousingly carrousingly
dragging the reluctant along
pell mel
helter skelter.
They grab stuff up
hold it
like a kitten
by the ruff
aloft
and glory in it—
that wonderfully superfluous stuff.

Midwinter Lambing
(Near Lukachukai Mountain, 1878)

Temperature excessive
oppressive
hardening afterbirth
and seeking on sand
bleats of life.

Busy hands of the reed clan
and night
like buzzards
beaten back for a time
by reeds afire.

Hands of burning skin
busy among bleats
and white piles
with frozen
shadows.

Ewes mixing milling
crying in the
frenzied frozen
time of tired
bone.

Copper touch of first
glow with no heat
though busy
on western mesas
with hope.

Among Sheep

Singing Sister in white muslin
among sheep
in a sandland of blowing colors
mostly reds.
Standing Horse's flank
a chant of beauty and meat
coyote track,
and a witch winter's teeth.
Singing Sister
a robe, a man, some calico
and slow the clouds —
    fat wethers —
and black the crow
toward the mesa.
Singing Sister quiet
among the flock
alive
in beauty.

In a Grey Suit

The gray mantis

grasps

with cold speed,

unfolding elongated appendages

fast,

preying on whatever passes,

neatly snacking.

Puffery

Surprisingly easily

I see a lizard

on a fence,

uncamouflaged,

arrogantly green

on gray,

mouth stretched

and full of prey,

puffed pouch

a bragging flag

of silver and red.

Flicking tail

and flashing eyes

advertise his fame

while a cricket

twitches

frenziedly

to an end.

www.ingramcontent.com/pod-product-compliance
Lightning Source LLC
Chambersburg PA
CBHW020523030426
42337CB00011B/520